Masters of Water-Colour Painting

H. M. Cundall

Originally Published by
THE STUDIO, LTD.
1922

INTRODUCTION

The earliest form of painting was with colours ground in water. Egyptian artists three thousand years B.C. used this method, and various mediums, such as wax and mastic, were added as a fixative. It was what is now known as tempera painting. The Greeks acquired their knowledge of the art from the Egyptians, and later the Romans dispersed it throughout Europe. They probably introduced tempera painting into this country for decoration of the walls of their houses. The English monks visited the Continent and learnt the art of miniature painting for illuminating their manuscripts by the same process. Owing to opaque white being mixed with the colours the term of painting in body-colour came in use. Painting in this manner was employed by artists throughout Europe in making sketches for their oil paintings.

Two such drawings by Albrecht Dürer, produced with great freedom in the early part of the sixteenth century, are in the British Museum. The Dutch masters also employed the same means. Holbein introduced the painting of miniature portraits into this country, for although the monks inserted figures in their illuminations, little attempt was made in producing likenesses. As early as the middle of the seventeenth century the term "water colours" came into use. In an inventory, in manuscript, of the personal estate of Charles I, which was sold by an Act of Parliament, numerous pictures are thus described.

Wenceslaus Hollar, a native of Prague, came to England in 1637, and became drawing-master to the Prince of Wales and the Duke of York. The painting of landscapes was first introduced by him into this country. He made topographical drawings with a reed pen, and afterwards added slight local colours. The earliest Englishman known to follow this style was Francis Barlow. He is principally noted for his drawings with a pen, slightly tinted, of animals and birds, with landscapes in the background. Later, Peter Monamy, a marine painter who was born in Jersey, produced drawings in a similar manner. Early in the eighteenth century Pieter Tillemans came to England, and painted hunting scenes, race-horses and country-seats. He worked in a free style in washes of colour without any outlines with a pen or underlying grey tints. To a "Natural History of Birds," by George Edwards, library keeper to the Royal College of Physicians, published in 1751, is added an appendix, entitled, "A Brief and General Idea of Drawing and Painting in

Water Colours: Intended for the amusement of the curious rather than the instruction of artists." In it he states, "There are two ways of painting in water colours: one by mixing white with your colours and laying on a thick body; the other is only washing your paper or vellum with a thin water tinctured with colour." After giving details of the methods to be employed he adds, "the former method of using water colours is called painting and the other washing or staining." During the latter half of the century it became a fashion for landed gentry to have engravings made of their country seats, and antiquarian publications with illustrations were produced. These created a demand for

topographical draughtsmen to assist the engravers. In the catalogues of the Exhibitions of the Society of Artists, the first of which was held in 1760, the drawings by these men are styled as being "stained," "tinted," or "washed."

The English School of Water-Colour Painting was now firmly established, and several artists have been claimed to be the "father" of it. Amongst them were William Tavener, an amateur painter, whose drawings were never topographically correct, as he exaggerated buildings to give them a classic appearance; Samuel Scott, a marine painter and styled the English Canaletto, he was called by Horace Walpole "the first painter of the age—one whose works will charm any age," and was also a friend of Hogarth; also Alexander Cozens, born in Russia and the reputed son of Peter the Great, but lately it has been suggested that Richard Cozens, a ship-builder, who went to Russia in 1700, may have been his father. He was sent to Italy to study art, and afterwards came to England. He professed to teach amateurs how to produce pictures without study. Edwards, in his "Anecdotes of Painting," describes his process as dashing out a number of accidental large blots and loose flourishes from which he selected forms and sometimes produced very grand ideas. Dayes called him "Blotmaster-general to the town."

The painter, however, who is most generally regarded as being the father of water-colour painting was Paul Sandby, R.A. He first obtained employment in the Military Drawing Office of the Tower of London. Afterwards he resided with his elder brother, Thomas Sandby, at Windsor. At first he painted in the usual tinted manner of the period, but later he worked with body-colour, by which manner he added considerable richness to his drawings. *Windsor Castle: View of the Round andDevil's Towers from the Black Rock* (Plate I) is an admirable example of his latter method. The drawing has been acquired through the Felton Bequest Fund, and now hangs in the National Gallery of Victoria. Paul Sandby was for many years the chief drawing-master at the Royal Military Academy at Woolwich. He was also appointed by George III to give instruction in drawing to his sons.

The work of Francis Towne has only of recent years come to be appreciated. He belonged to a Devonshire family, but the exact place of his birth is not known. He became a friend of William Pars, A.R.A., from whom he received some instruction in drawing, and also went with him to Rome in 1780.

Although he spent considerable time on the Continent, numerous drawings by him exist of scenes in his native country. *Onthe Dart* (Plate II) is a good example of his delicate method of painting. His special skill lay "in the management of even pen-line and in a subtle modulation of colour upon a flat surface."

Amongst the early topographical men was Michael (Angelo) Rooker, A.R.A. The additional Christian name is said to have been given to him by Paul Sandby, under whom he studied for some time. He made pedestrian tours through England, and executed a large number of drawings, which are remarkable for their accuracy and delicate treatment, such as the *Village Scene* (Plate III).

Thomas Hearne was a contemporary with Rooker. It was a custom at this period for topographical artists to travel abroad with British Embassies to foreign countries and with Governors to Colonial possessions. Photography had not yet been invented, and the drawings by these artists were the only means by which the majority of inhabitants of this island were able to obtain some idea of places beyond the sea. Hearne went to the Leeward Isles, as draughtsman to the Governor, and produced records of the scenery there. Afterwards he executed a number of drawings in this country, some of which were engraved in "Antiquities of Great Britain." *View of Gloucester* (Plate IV) is an example of his accurate drawing, though somewhat weak in colouring. Joseph Farington, R.A., received instruction in drawing from Wilson, and his paintings show slight evidence of it, as may be seen from the *Scotch Landscape* (Plate V), but he simply copied Nature without enduing his work with any of his master's poetic reeling. Thomas Malton, Junr., was noted for the accuracy with which he drew architectural views, many of them being street scenes in London, and they are of considerable value as records. *Old Palace Yard, Westminster* (Plate VI) is interesting as showing buildings on the north side of Henry VII's Chapel of the Abbey, which have long since been demolished. He published works aquatinted by himself, including *Westminster*, which appeared in 1792. He held classes at which Girtin and Turner attended. The latter used to say, "My early master was Tom Malton." Edward Dayes was a versatile artist; he painted architectural subjects, into which he frequently introduced figures, such as *Furness Abbey* (Plate VII), executed miniatures and engraved in mezzotint. He also wrote several works on art. *Buckingham House, St.James's Park*, in which a number of the *beau monde* are seen promenading in the park, is one of his best paintings. An engraving of it by F. D. Soiron, produced in 1793, under the title of *Promenade in St. James's Park*, was very popular.

Francis Wheatley, R.A., was a topographical artist, but is better known as a painter of *genre* subjects, especially by the engravings after "The Cries of London." *Preparing for Market* (Plate VIII) is a good example of his latter work, which was somewhat insipid.

The reputation of Thomas Rowlandson, who could paint landscapes with great ability, rests upon his caricatures, which were usually drawn in outline and tinted. He lived a somewhat dissipated life, and possessed an abundant sense of humour, as displayed in the *Entrance to VauxhallGardens* (Plate IX), the noted place of amusement and rendezvous of the fashionable set in the early part of the last century.

John Robert Cozens, the son of Alexander Cozens, was the first artist at this period "to break away from the trammels of topography, and to raise landscape painting in water colours to a branch of fine art." He travelled abroad and studied principally in Italy and Switzerland. The lake of Nemi, situated in the Campagna, some sixteen miles west of Rome, and reached by the famous Via Appia, has always been a favourite subject with both poets and artists. Near the north rim of the worn-out crater, in which the lake is situated, is the village of Nemi, surmounted by a fine old castle, which passed through the hands of many noble families. Pope, Byron, and others have sung the praises of the lake. Turner has left at least five drawings of it, one of which is engraved in Hakewell's "Italy." William Pars, Richard Wilson and other artists of the early landscape school also painted the scene. Cozens made many drawings of Nemi and the vicinity. Two are in the Victoria and Albert Museum and another is in the Whitworth Institute, Manchester. The painting (Plate X), belonging to Mr. R. W. Lloyd, shows the lake with Palazzo Cesarini on a height by its side, and the Campagna in the distance. It is a fine example of Cozens' work treated in his poetic manner, and into which more colour than usual has been introduced. Cozens' last visit to Italy was made in 1782 in company with the noted William Beckford, the author of "Vathek." On his return he gradually lost his reason. It is pathetic to think such was the sad end of a man inspired with such artistic talents. As it has already been stated, he was the pioneer in exalting water-colour painting to a fine art. His footsteps were quickly followed by Girtin and Turner. The history of these two artists, how during their early struggles they were befriended by that art patron, Dr. Thomas Monro, a capable water-colour painter himself, and well qualified to give advice, is too well known to need repetition.

Girtin, during his short career, had no selfish ideas of keeping his knowledge of painting to himself. It was mainly due to his initiation that a club was started amongst a small body of young artists for the study of landscape painting. They met at each other's houses in rotation. One of its prominent members was Sir Robert Ker Porter, a painter, traveller and author, who afterwards married a Russian princess. He was living, at the time, at 16, Great Newport Street, which had formerly been a residence of Sir Joshua Reynolds, and subsequently that of Dr. Samuel Johnson. It was in this house that the first meeting of the club was held "for the purpose of establishing by practice a School of Historic Landscape, the subjects being designs from poetick passages." Writing in *The Somerset House Gazette*, in 1823, W. H. Pyne, under the pseudonym of Ephraim Hardcastle, states "this artist (Girtin) prepared his drawings on the same principle which had hitherto been confined to painting in oil, namely, with local colour, and shadowing the same with the individual tint of its own shadow. Previous to the practice of Turner and Girtin, drawings were shadowed first entirely throughout, whatever their component parts—houses, castles, trees, mountains, foregrounds, middle-grounds, and distances, all with black or grey, and these objects were afterwards stained or tinted, enriched and finished, as is now the custom to colour prints. It was this new practice, introduced by these distinguished artists, that acquired for designs in water colour upon paper the title of paintings: a designation which many works of the existing school decidedly merit, as we lately beheld in the Exhibition of the Painters in Water Colours, where pictures of this class were displayed in gorgeous frames, bearing out in effect against the mass of glittering gold as powerfully as pictures in oil." Girtin had a partiality for

painting in a low tone of colour and frequently on rough cartridge paper, which assisted in giving a largeness of manner to his work. The *Landscape* (Plate XI) is, however, rendered in a brighter key than his usual practice.

As limitation of space will not admit of giving any account of the life of Turner, already well known, it may be sufficient to say that *Lucerne: Moonlight* (Plate XII) was painted in 1843, and was originally in the collection of Mr. H. A. J. Munro of Novar. Ruskin, who calls it a noble drawing in his "Notes on his Drawings by the late J. M. W. Turner," makes a mistake in the title and describes it as *Zurich byMoonlight.* John Sell Cotman, a member of the Norwich School, was another pioneer who did much for the advancement of water-colour painting. Unfortunately, his work was not appreciated during his career. If he had lived in the twentieth century he would have had no cause for the fits of depression to which he was subject during the greater part of life. It can be well recognised that in the first half of last century the public, who were mainly accustomed to carefully drawn topographical scenes, failed to appreciate such paintings as the *Classical Scene* (Plate XIII), executed with such freedom and vigour. It was recently exhibited at the Special Exhibition of Cotman's Paintings at the Tate Gallery, when five other classical landscape compositions were also shown. Cotman's work was not understood. His paintings, both in oil and water colour, often only realised less than a pound apiece. He was compelled to resort to teaching in order to support his family. Eventually, through the influence of his friend, Lady Palgrave, and the strong support of Turner, he obtained the post of drawing-master at King's College School, London. His position then became more secure. Still, teaching boys in the underground rooms of Somerset House could not have been inspiriting to one who yearned to seek Nature in the open air. He could not exclaim, like "Old" Crome, when he with his pupils was once met on the banks of the Yare, "This is our academy." He died of a broken heart. At the beginning of the nineteenth century there was a feeling amongst the artists who worked solely in water colours that they were not being fairly treated by the Royal Academy. They were ineligible to be elected members of that body, and they were of opinion that their works were never placed in a prominent position on the walls of the galleries. William Frederick Wells, a friend of Turner and said to have suggested to him the idea of producing his "Liber Studiorum," proposed to his fellow artists that they should form a separate society for the promotion of water-colour painting. After considerable negotiations, ten artists met together in November, 1804, and founded the Society of Painters in Water Colours. The first exhibition was held in the Spring of the following year at rooms in Lower Brook Street. After various vicissitudes and many changes of abode this society, known in later years as the "Old" Society, eventually obtained a lease of the premises in Pall Mall East. Thus, after much roving for seventeen years, a permanent home was secured, and the centenary of the occupation of these galleries has just been completed. Varley and Glover were two of the original members.

De Wint, Copley Fielding, David Cox and Samuel Prout were subsequently elected Associates, and afterwards became full members.

Amongst the founders the name of John Varley stands out beyond the others. He was born at Hackney (see Plate XIV) in 1778. Receiving but little instruction in art besides the assistance given to him by Dr. Monro, he became a teacher of considerable reputation. Amongst his pupils were many who afterwards became famous. To mention only a few, there were William Mulready, who married his sister, Copley Fielding, who espoused his wife's sister, W. Turner (of Oxford), David Cox, William H. Hunt, Oliver Finch and John Linnell. Varley was a prolific worker, and contributed more than seven hundred drawings to the "Old" Society, averaging about forty works annually. His style was broad and simple, with tints beautifully laid, without resort to stippling. He wrote some works on drawing and perspective. He also was an enthusiast in astrology, and compiled a "Treatise on Zodiacal Physiognomy." John Glover was a landscape painter and produced works, both in oil and in water colours, into which he frequently introduced cattle. His father having been a small farmer may account for this partiality for animals. In water-colour painting he followed the methods of William Payne, the inventor of a grey tint known as Payne's grey, in producing foliage by splitting the hairs of his brush in order to give a feeling of lightness, and he was partial to sunlight effects (see Plate XV). He was President of the "Old" Society on two occasions, but he resigned his membership, so as to become eligible for election to the Royal Academy. He failed in his object and joined the Society of British Artists. Glover suddenly left England in 1831, and went to the Swan River Settlement in Australia. Afterwards he removed to Tasmania, where he died.

Peter De Wint, a descendant of an old merchant family of Amsterdam, like Glover, painted in oils and water colours, but his work was far superior. He selected broad and open country for his scenes, which were executed in a rich tone with a tendency to heavy uniform green. The neighbourhood of

Lincoln, where his wife, a sister of W. Hilton, R.A., was born, had special attractions to him. *St. Albans* (Plate XVI) shows the abbey in the ruinous state it had become from the time of the Reformation. Its restoration was not commenced until 1856, under the direction of Sir Gilbert Scott, and completed later by Lord Grimthorpe. Anthony Vandyke Copley Fielding belonged to an artistic family. His father was a painter and three of his brothers all practised art with success. He was one of the most fashionable drawing-masters of his day, and a strong supporter of the "Old" Society. After being treasurer and next secretary, he was appointed president in 1831, which post he retained during his life. He was a most prolific worker and contributed about seventeen hundred drawings to the Society's exhibitions, besides showing at the Royal Academy and Royal Institution. At first his favourite subjects were lake and mountain scenery (see Plate XVII). After he took up his residence at Brighton he turned his attention to marine painting and depicted many storms at sea. It has been exaggeratedly said that Copley Fielding was "perhaps the greatest artist after Turner for representations of breadth and atmosphere." Ruskin also praised his work. Owing, however, to his very rapid method of execution there was a considerable sameness in his work.

The drawings by David Cox, although executed in an apparently careless manner, give a greater rendering of atmospheric qualities and of irradiation of light with a feeling of more movement than can be found in the works of Fielding. Cox's early drawings were executed in a somewhat stiff and restrained manner, with a delicate finish, but afterwards his style became broad and he produced those breezy effects which are almost unrivalled. *Boys Fishing* (Plate XVIII) is an excellent example of his later work. When Cox returned to his native town, Birmingham, he devoted his attention to working in oils, and the City Art Gallery possesses a superb collection of his paintings in this medium. He was for the greater part of his life a teacher of drawing, and he published a "Treatise on Landscape Painting and Effect in Water Colours," in which his views are clearly stated.*

Samuel Prout, one of the numerous Devonshire painters, also derived a great part of his income by giving instruction in drawing and painting. Numerous drawing copies for students were produced by him by means of soft-ground etching. He was at first employed by John Britton, the author of "The Beauties of England and Wales," in making topographical drawings for this work. In 1819 he went to Normandy for the benefit of his health. There he turned his attention to producing those paintings of cathedrals and picturesque buildings for which he is noted. Later he travelled through Germany and Switzerland to Italy, and visited Rome and Venice (see Plate XIX). Afterwards he published facsimiles of many of the drawings executed during these tours on the Continent. They were produced in lithography by himself on the stone, an art in which he greatly excelled. The architectural drawings by Prout are remarkable for their picturesque treatment, rather than for correctness of construction. Details are sparsely indicated by the use of a reed pen. Bright effects of light and shade are, however, given, and the introduction of groups of figures add brilliancy to these paintings.

James Duffield Harding, like Prout, from whom he received some lessons, also excelled in lithography. Many of his paintings were reproduced by him in a publication entitled "Sketches at Home and Abroad." He visited Italy on two occasions. *Vico, in the Bay ofNaples*, between Castellamare and Sorrento (Plate XX), is an example of his free manner of painting. An engraving of it appeared in the "Landscape Annual" in 1832. He was a member of the "Old" Society, and also painted in oils. William Henry Hunt, familiarly called "Old" or "Billy" Hunt in his latter years by his fellow artists, to distinguish him from William Holman Hunt, was an artist with a style peculiar to himself. He painted figures, especially young rustics, with a sense of humour, but he is chiefly noted for his exquisite fruit and flower pieces, which were executed with great delicacy and with a remarkable power of rendering the effects of light and shade on the surface of the objects. To obtain these he would

roughly pencil out, say, a group of plums, and thickly coat each one with Chinese white, which would be left to harden. On this ground he afterwards painted his colours with a sure hand. By this means he would obtain a brilliant effect. Further, to enhance it, he would make free use of the knife on the various surroundings to give a contrast, and at the same time to produce a feeling of texture on the various surfaces, so as not to have a monotonous and flat appearance. This method of scraping up portions of the surface of the paper is clearly shown in *Plucking the Fowl* (Plate XXI).

James Holland commenced his artistic career by painting flowers on pottery at the factory of James Davenport at Burslem. He came to London and continued to paint flowers. After a visit to Paris he devoted himself to landscapes. Subsequently he visited Venice, and produced, in both oils and water colours, some excellent paintings remarkable for their brilliant colouring (see Plate XXII).

James Baker Pyne, born at Bristol, was a self-taught artist. He also is noted for his brilliant colouring, but there is a want of solidity in his painting. He visited the Continent and travelled as far as Italy (see Plate XXIII). His landscapes were chiefly river and lake subjects. He published "The English Lake District" and "The Lake Scenery of England," illustrated with lithographs of his works. He was a member of the Society of British Artists, and became a vice-president. Like Girtin, the illustrious young painter Richard Parkes Bonington was cut off in life at the early age of twenty-seven. He was born at Arnold, near Nottingham. Whilst still a boy he was taken by his parents to Calais, where he received some instruction in water colours from Francia. Later the family settled in Paris. Here Bonington resided the greater part of his life. He made a few visits to England, and on the last occasion he was taken ill and died of consumption. He practised at the Louvre and the *Institut*, and also received instruction from Baron

Gros. His paintings, in oil and water colours, were almost entirely executed in France; he, however, made one visit to Italy. In Paris his works were chiefly architectural with street scenes, admirably executed, whilst his landscapes with fine atmospheric effects (see Plate XXIV) display great freedom in execution. It is somewhat remarkable that after Cotman and Bonington had, in the first part of the nineteenth century, developed a style so greatly appreciated at the present time, so many of the landscape painters in water colours in the early Victorian era should still have adhered to the old restricted methods. Constable exercised considerable influence on the French landscape painting in oil, whilst Bonington showed the French artists the capabilities of water colours, which they did not fail to appreciate.

H. M. Cundall.

The "Treatise" has recently been republished as the Special Autumn Number of *The Studio.*

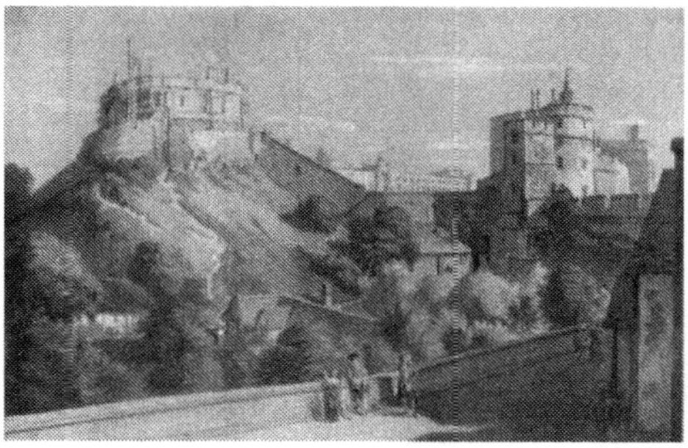

PLATE I
"WINDSOR CASTLE: VIEW OF THE ROUND AND DEVIL'S TOWERS FROM THE BLACK ROCK"
BY PAUL SANDBY, R.A.
(Size, 11¾ × 17¼ IN.)
(*Acquired by the National Art Gallery of Victoria, Melbourne*)

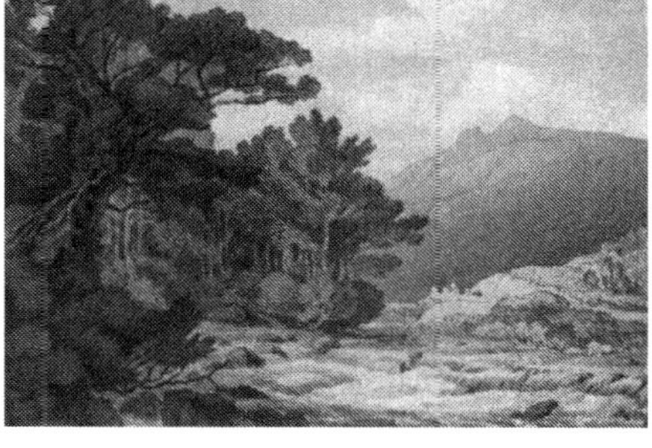

PLATE II
"ON THE DART"
BY FRANCIS TOWNE
(Size, 7 × 9¾ IN.)
(In the possession of A. E. Hutton, Esq.)

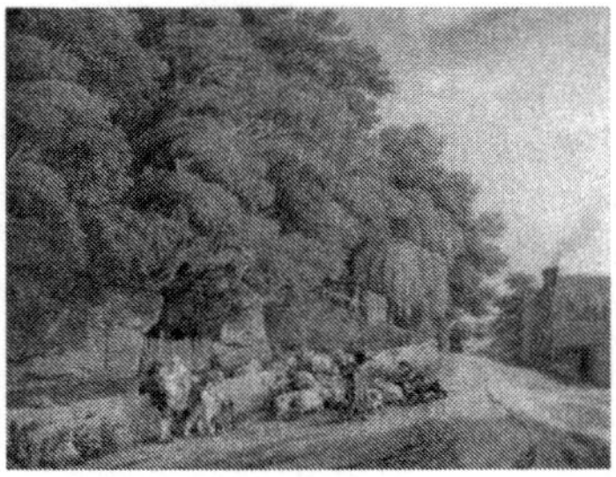

PLATE III
"VILLAGE SCENE"
BY MICHAEL (ANGELO) ROOKER, A.R.A.
(Size, 14½ × 18¼ IN.)
(In the possession of Victor Rienaecker, Esq.)

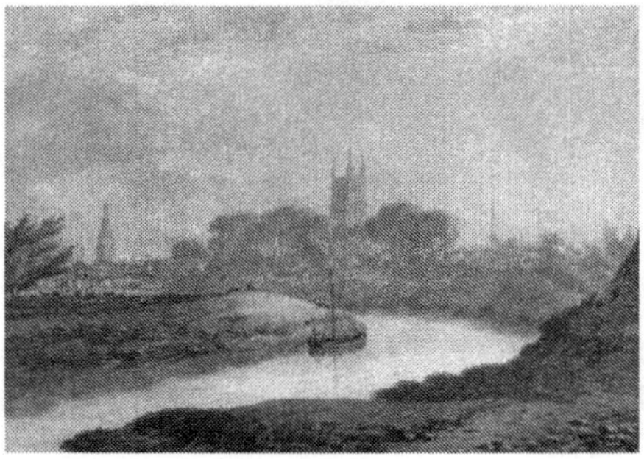

PLATE IV
"VIEW OF GLOUCESTER"
BY THOMAS HEARNE
(Size, 7½ × 10½ IN.)
(In the possession of Victor Rienaecker, Esq.)

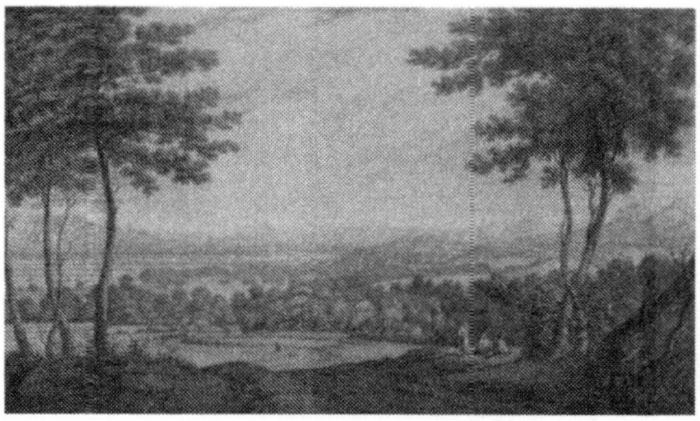

PLATE V
"SCOTCH LANDSCAPE"
BY JOSEPH FARINGTON, R.A.
(Size, 20¾ × 33¾ IN.)
(In the possession of Victor Rienaecker, Esq.)

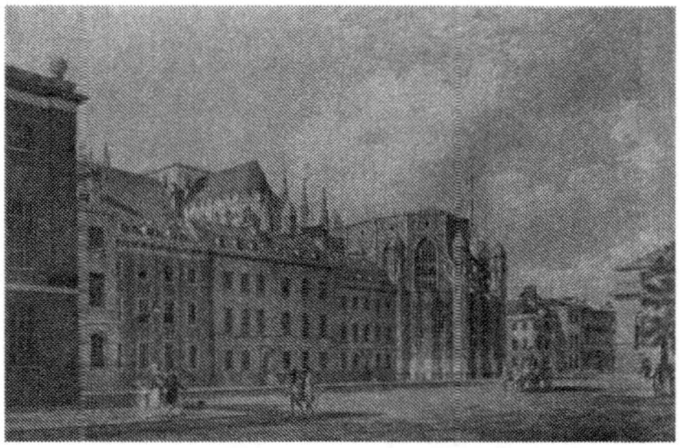

PLATE VI
"OLD PALACE YARD, WESTMINSTER,"
BY THOMAS MALTON, JUN.
(Size, 13 × 19 IN.)
(In the possession of R. W. Lloyd, Esq.)

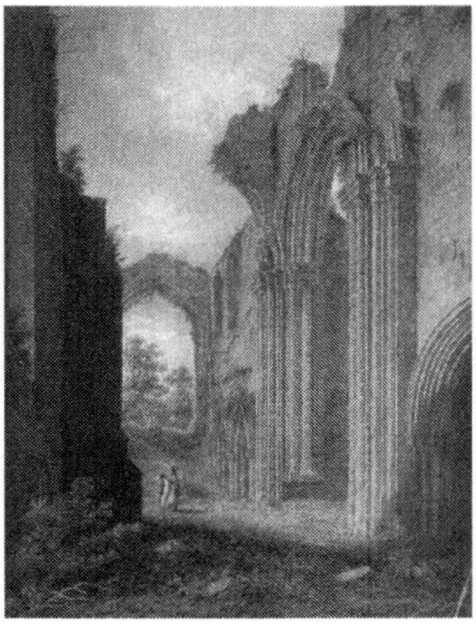

PLATE VII
"FURNESS ABBEY, LANCASHIRE"
BY EDWARD DAYES
(Size, 27½ × 20¾ IN.)
(In the possession of Victor Rienaecker, Esq.)

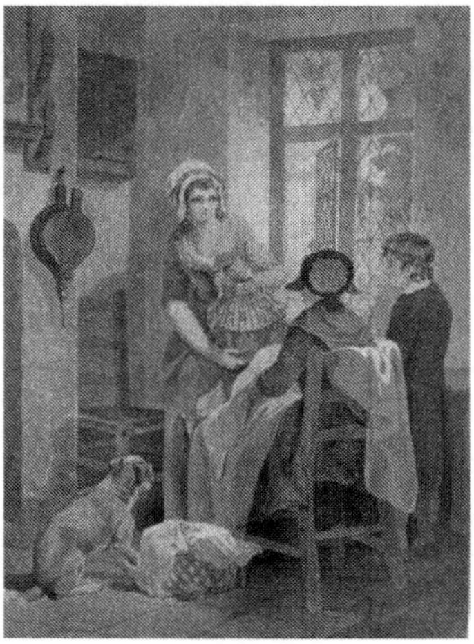

PLATE VIII
"PREPARING FOR MARKET"
BY FRANCIS WHEATLEY, R.A.,
(Size, 14 × 10 IN.)
(In the possession of Messrs. Thos. Agnew & Sons)

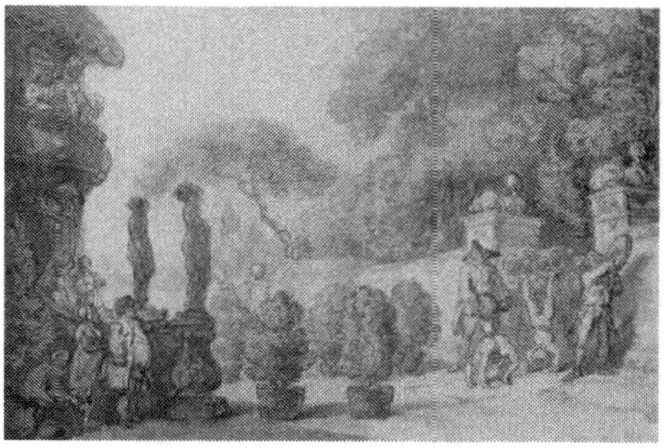

PLATE IX
"ENTRANCE TO VAUXHALL GARDENS"
BY THOMAS ROWLANDSON
(Size, 9 × 12? IN.)
(*In the possession of Victor Rienaecker, Esq.*)

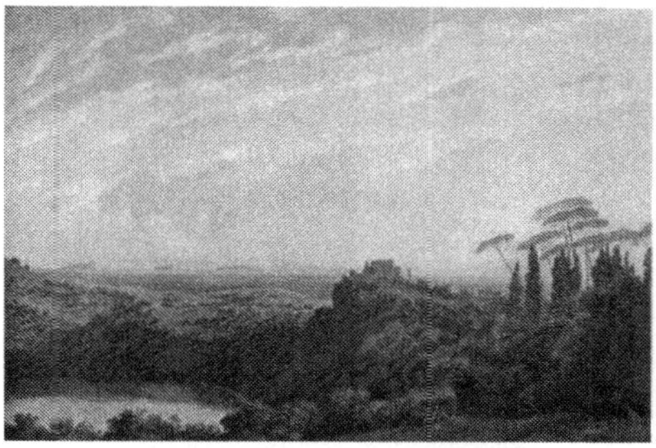

PLATE X
"LAKE NEMI"
BY JOHN ROBERT COZENS
(Size, 14½ × 21 IN.)
(*In the possession of R. W. Lloyd, Esq.*)

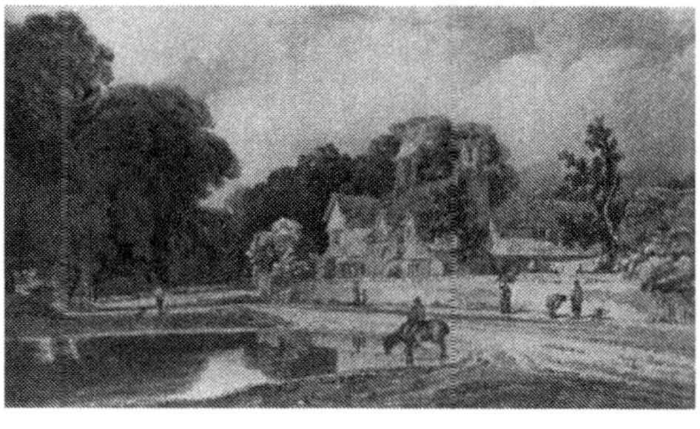

PLATE XI
LANDSCAPE
BY THOMAS GIRTIN
(Size, 12¼ × 20½ IN)
(*In the possession of R. W. Lloyd, Esq.*)

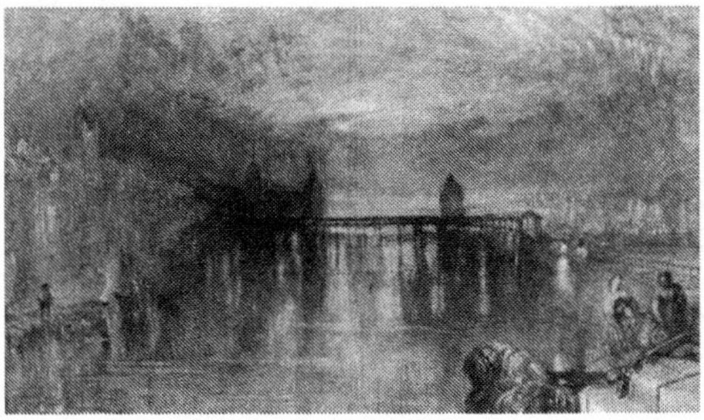

PLATE XII
"LUCERNE: MOONLIGHT"
BY J. M. W. TURNER, R.A.
(Size, 11½ × 18¾ IN.)
(*In the possession of R. W. Lloyd, Esq.*)

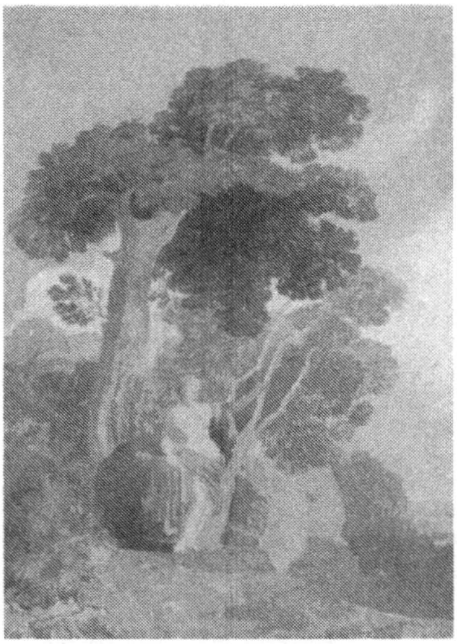

PLATE XIII
"CLASSICAL SCENE"
BY JOHN SELL COTMAN
(Size, 11½ × 8¼ IN.)

(*In the possession of G. Bellingham Smith, Esq.*)

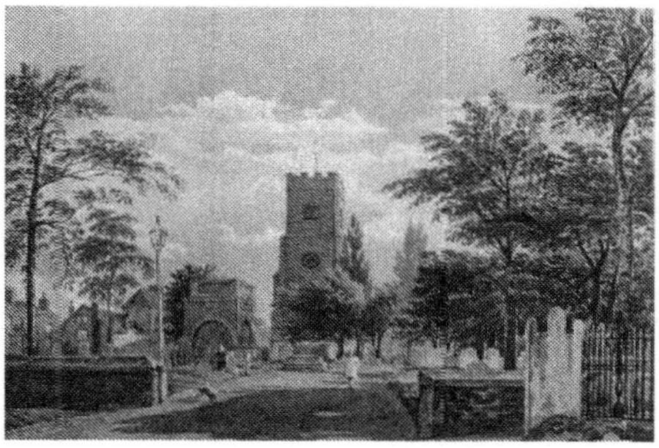

PLATE XIV
"HACKNEY CHURCH"
BY JOHN VARLEY
(Size, 11 × 15 IN.)
(*In the possession of R. W. Lloyd, Esq.*)

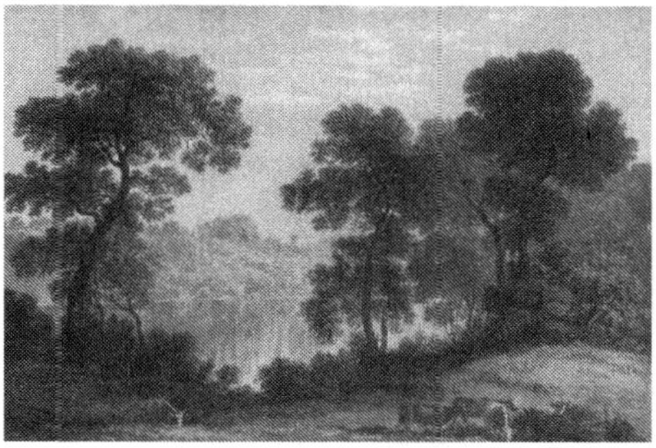

PLATE XV
"VIEW IN NORTH WALES"
BY JOHN GLOVER
(Size, 16? × 23 IN.)
(*In the possession of Victor Rienaecker, Esq.*)

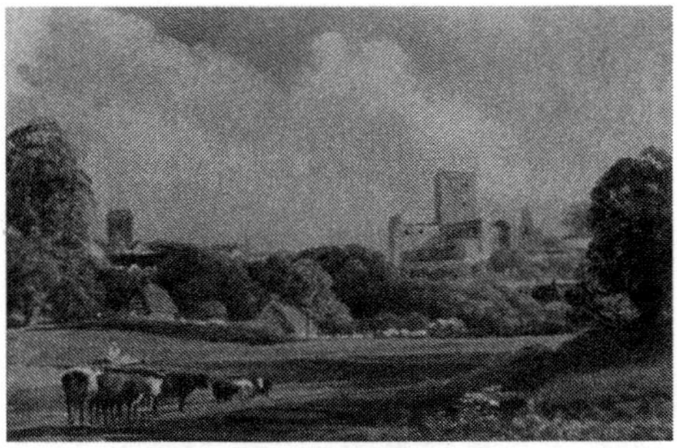

PLATE XVI
"ST. ALBANS"
BY PETER DE WINT
(Size, 9¾ × 14½ IN.)
(In the possession of R. W. Lloyd, Esq.)

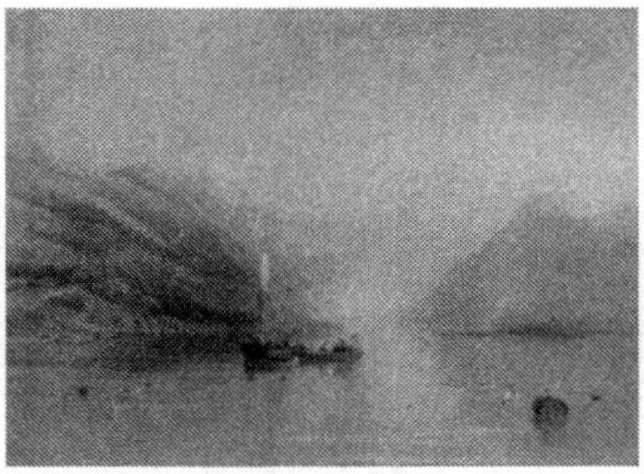

PLATE XVII
"LAKE SCENE"
BY A. V. COPLEY FIELDING
(Size, 12¼ × 16? IN.)
(In the Possession of Victor Rienaecker, Esq.)

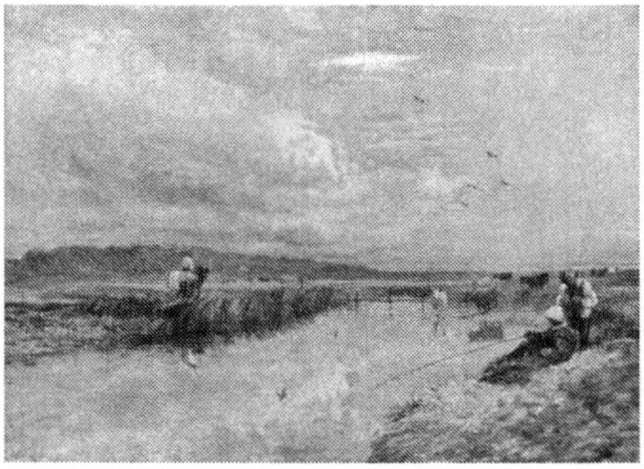

PLATE XVIII

"BOYS FISHING"
BY DAVID COX
(Size, 10½ × 14½ IN.)
(In the possession of R. W. Lloyd, Esq.)

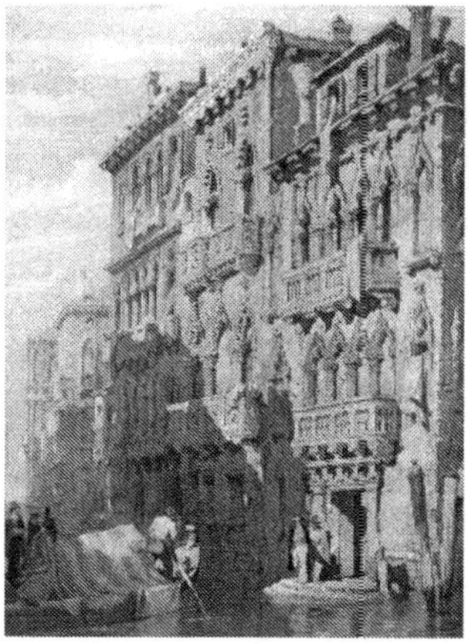

PLATE XIX
"PALAZZO CONTARINI FASAN
ON THE GRAND CANAL, VENICE"
BY SAMUEL PROUT
(Size, 16? × 11½ IN.)
(In the Victoria and Albert Museum)

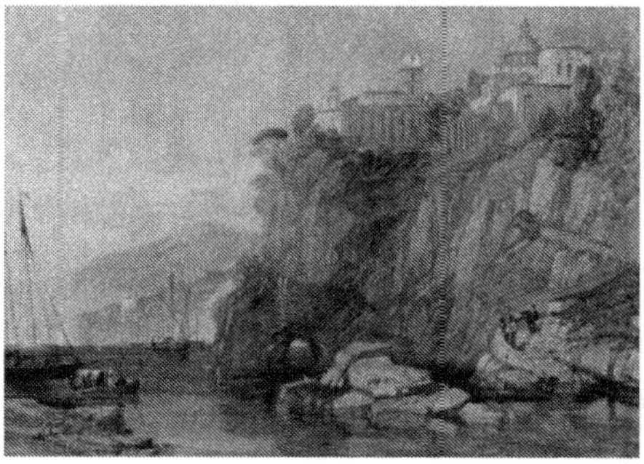

PLATE XX
"VICO, BAY OF NAPLES"
BY JAMES DUFFIELD HARDING
(Size, 8½ × 11¾ IN.)
(In the possession of Victor Rienaecker, Esq.)

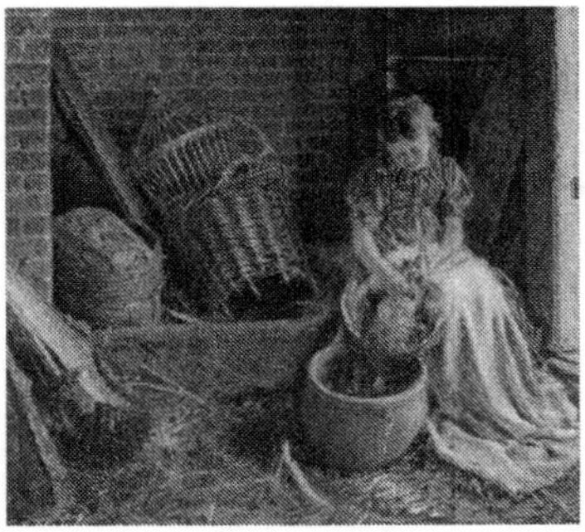

PLATE XXI
"PLUCKING THE FOWL"
BY WILLIAM HENRY HUNT
(Size, 13¾ × 14½ IN.)
(*In the possession of R. W. Lloyd, Esq.*)

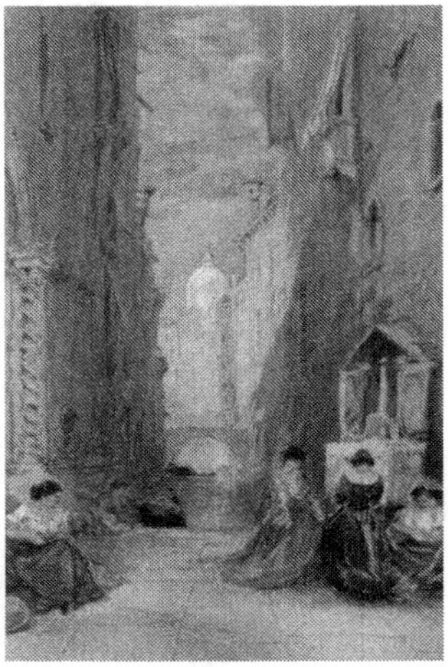

PLATE XXII
"A SHRINE IN VENICE"
BY JAMES HOLLAND
(Size, 9¾ × 6½ IN.)
(*In the possession of Victor Rienaecker, Esq.*)

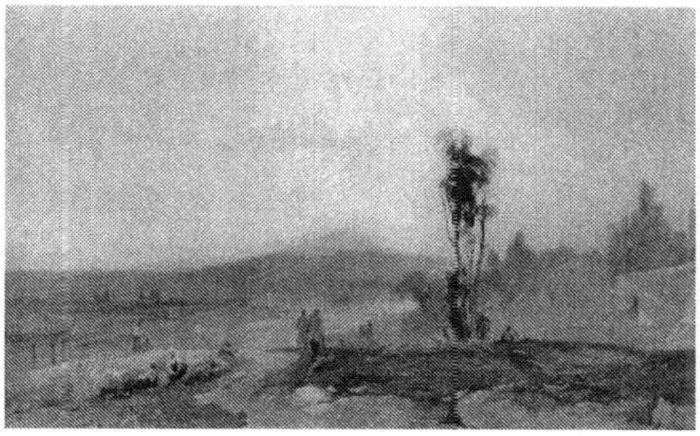

PLATE XXIII
"VIEW IN ITALY"
BY JAMES BAKER PYNE
(Size, 10¾ × 17 IN.)
(In the possession of R. W. Lloyd, Esq.)

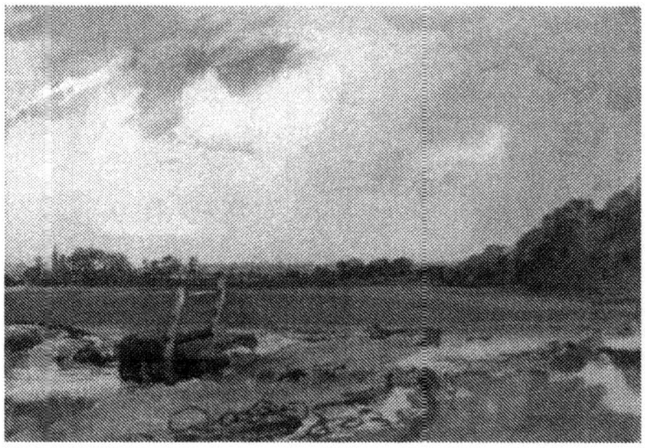

PLATE XXIV
"NEAR JUMIEGES"
BY RICHARD PARKES BONINGTON
(Size, 8¾ × 12¼ IN.)
(In the possession of Messrs. Thos. Agnew & Sons)

www.ingramcontent.com/pod-product-compliance
Lightning Source LLC
Chambersburg PA
CBHW071717130725
29531CB00036B/1720